American Kestrel
The Diminutive Raptor

Written and Illustrated by Scott Rashid
Published by Scott Rashid

This book may be purchased from the author, or from Amazon
Scott Rashid
Box 3351
Estes Park, CO. 80517
E-mail: srashid@carriep.org
Website: www.carriep.org

American Kestrel

The Diminutive Raptor

By:

Scott Rashid

Dedication:

In Memory of

Dr. Ronald Ryder

Acknowledgements:

I would like to thank the following individuals for their contribution to this project.

Thomas Andersen, Paul Avante, Carol Cochran, Gina Digillianardo, Ann Donohue, John Donovan, Debbie Ely, Gary Eyers, Rick Hagman, Michelle van Hare, Cliff Hendrick, Catherine Jepson, Larry Kilgore, Cliff Malone, Kristin Oles, Joe Piombino, Pam Piombino, Jon Rayeski, Lauren Sadowski, Mike Sherman, Debra Sherill, Rick Spowart, Mary Thacker, Jim Tolstrup and Steve Vandenberg

American Kestrel

The Diminutive Raptor

Contents

Introduction

According to the America Kestrel Partnership; American Kestrel numbers have been in decline for many years due to a loss of habitat and nesting sites, predation and desease.

American Kestrels, previously known as Sparrow Hawks, are secondary cavity nesting birds of prey. Which means that they need to nest in a cavity, but are uable to construct one themselves. They feed upon small vertebrates and insects.

From the 1940's to the 1990's, when DDT was in use, American Kestrel numbers declined due to their egg shells becoming too thin to withstand the weight of the female during incubation. When a female sat on her eggs, the eggs were crushed. After DDT was discontinued, and researchers began building and placing nest boxes for American Kestrels, their numbers began to increase. After the 1990's, fewer and fewer nest boxes were being built and placed for American Kestrels.

With the combination of lack of nesting sites, and the influx of West Nile Virus, a few years later. American Kestrels numbers began declinging again. In many areas have yet to rebound. Knowing this, members of the Colorado Avian Research and Rehabilitation Institiute, or CARRI, began building and placing nest boxes for American Kestrels 2018. We have placed live cameras inside several of these nest boxes to monitor the birds' nesting activities in real time.

Within the pages of **American Kestrel**, *The Diminuative Raptor*, you will read about the natural history of this colorful predator and the work we do to help increase their numbers.

Adult Male American Kestrel

Nine day old American Kestrel nestling

Chapter One

The American Kestrel Project

According to the American Kestrel Partnership, kestrel.peregrinefund.org/decline. American Kestrels have declined throughout North America, at a rate of between, 6% to more than 30%, from the 1960's to 2010. This decline is due primarily to human impact including loss of habitat and nesting sites, window crashes, being hit by cars and wind turbines, and pesticides. Predation and disease also play a role.

Knowing and seeing this in real time, gave me the idea to begin the American Kestrel Nest Box Project, in 2018. The project consists of building and placing nest boxes for American Kestrels and studying their nesting habits.

As of the spring of 2020, volunteers have built and placed more than 70 nest boxes for American Kestrels throughout Northern Colorado, with a goal of having 200 nest boxes in place as soon as we can find locations for them. The only hindrance, is finding landowners that will allow us to place nest boxes on their properties. Many people have never heard of the American Kestrel, which makes it hard for them to understand the importance of placing a nest box on their property. What works best is simply word-of-mouth. When we began the project, we reached out to family and friends who had property with good Kestrel habitat. After the boxes were placed, and birds began nesting, our friends began telling their friends about the project. Then those individuals with good American Kestrel habitat began contacting us about placing nest boxes on their properties.

Another way that we have expanded the project is to give presentations about Kestrels to various Audubon chapters and other birding groups. The more people that began hearing about the project, the more individuals wanted boxes. I also contacted a friend that works for Colorado Parks and Wildlife (CPW). CPW owns several properties throughout the state, many of which are perfect for this project. CPW also donated the wood that we used to construct the boxes that were placed on their properties. It is a great partnership. We are also partnering with the cities of Loveland, Superior and Louisville in placing nest boxes for Kestrels on their properties.

When we find locations that have both power and WiFi, we place Nest cameras® in the nest boxes. The cameras enable us to monitor the nesting cycles of the Kestrels in real time. These cameras can be watched on our website at www.carriep.org.

As of 2020, we have four American Kestrel nest boxes with Nest ®cameras inside. One of these nests is on the south side of a garage in Loveland. On the north side of the same structure is a much larger nest box for Barn Owls. We have cameras both inside and outside of that box and we have yet to witness any interaction between the American Kestrels and Barn Owls.

As of 2020, we have more than 30 nest boxes placed for Barn Owls. We have found that when we have good habitat for Barn Owls, we also have good, if not great, habitat for American Kestrels, as both species prefer like habitat and frequently feed on similar prey. Barn Owls normally begin nesting earlier than American Kestrels, but because Barn Owls frequently remain within their nests for more than 90 days and the American Kestrels remaining in their nests for roughly 60 days; the two species are frequently nesting simultaneously.

Using cameras as a research tool enables us to witness aspects of these birds' life cycle that would be impossible to observe without cameras. For example, we quickly learned that American Kestrels in Colorado begin looking at nest sites in March. Thus, in order to have the greatest success with Kestrels using our boxes they need to be in place before March. We like to have them in place ready for the birds by the end of January, to be safe.

Another thing that having cameras in the nest boxes showed us was, whether we were making the boxes the proper size for the Kestrels to comfortably raise their families. When I first began constructing nest boxes for Kestrels, in the early 1990's, they were eight-inches wide by eight-inches wide by twelve-inches deep, and had a roof barely overhung the front of the box. The entrance hole was three-inches in diameter.

After placing one of these boxes on a property in Loveland, the Kestrels ended up being predated by a raccoon. The raccoon climbed the pole, sat on top of the box and simply reached inside, grasped the entire family and ate them while sitting on top of the box. I decided to add a longer roof that would overhang the nest entrance by three-inches, but did not think of enlarging the box.

After the camera was placed in our first box, we quickly realized that the box was too small as the Kestrels appeared very crowded inside. We have since enlarged our boxes to eleven-inches wide by eleven inches wide by sixteen inches deep. Each box still has a three inch entrance hole, and roofs that overhang the front of each box three inches. This design ensures that no predators can reach the birds within our boxes.

When working with anything in nature, it is helpful to understand what species may predate your subject. Even birds of prey are vulnerable to predation when the young are inexperienced. Being sympathetic to this; we try not to place our American Kestrel nest boxes in areas were larger birds of prey are nesting. Cooper's Hawks and Great Horned Owls are predators of the tiny falcons, especially after the young have recently fledged and are not yet agile fliers. Therefore, many of our boxes are placed in more rural locations, often miles from housing developments. This ensures that the fledglings will not be predated by hawks and owls before they master the art of flight.

A large part of this project is to identify the individual Kestrels. The best way to do that is to place a numbered U.S. Geological Service leg band on each bird.

Being a licensed bird bander, enables me to legally band birds. I order the bands from the Bird Banding Laboratory in Maryland. When I can capture birds within their nest boxes, I place consecutively numbered leg bands on each nestling and any adults that are captured. After each bird is banded, I write down the location where the bird was banded along with the species, age and their sex. The information is sent to the Bird Banding Laboratory. When a banded bird is recovered, the information about the recovery is sent to the Bird Banding Laboratory, and they forward the information on to me. This enables me to identify individual birds and gain insight into nest site fidelity, longevity and mortality; provided one of the banded bird is either recaptured or found dead.

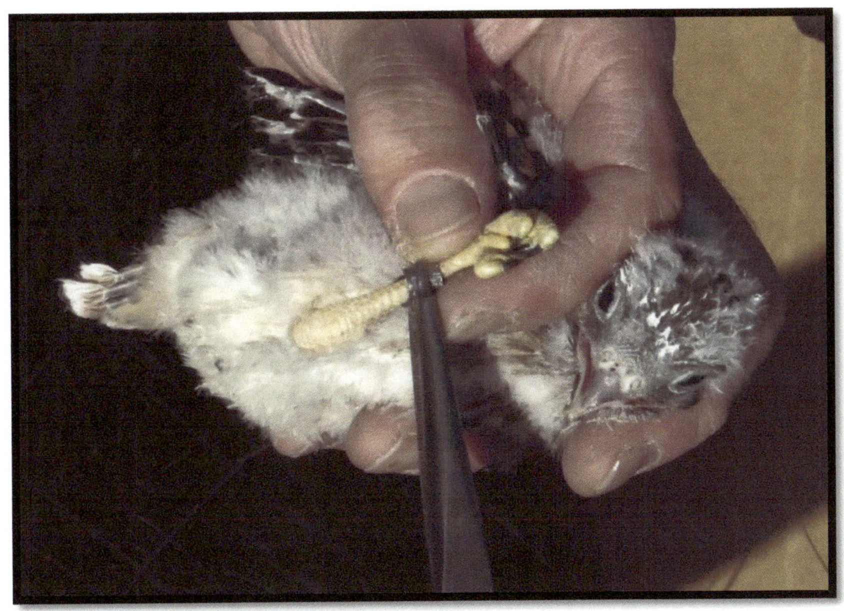

The author placing a band on a nestling American Kestrel (above)
Recently banded nestling female American Kestrel (below)

Cooper's Hawks (above) and Great Horned Owls (below) occasionally predate Kestrels

Chapter Two

The Anatomy of a Falcon:

There are fifteen species of Kestrel world-wide, but only one the American Kestrel nests in North America. American Kestrel is both the only North American falcon that nests in cavities and the smallest falcon on North America.

Like their larger cousin, the Merlin, American Kestrels are sexually dimorphic, in both size and color. Male Kestrels measure eight and ten inches from head to tail, and weigh between two and five ounces. The larger female Kestrels are between nine and twelve-inches and weigh between three and six-ounces.

Male Kestrels have slate blue-gray wings and spotted breasts. Female Kestrels have rust-colored wings and streaked breasts and bellies. Males have rusty tails with black bands with white tips; females have barred tails. Both sexes have dark vertical streaks below their eyes called malar stripes. These stripes may help to conceal the bird's eyes and reduce glare, like wearing sun glasses; as many falcon species spend much of their time perched in the open.

Falcons have long pointed wings and long tails. They also have large forward facing, dark brown eyes, often appearing black. Falcons have an orbital ring around each eye which deflects wind when the birds are diving at high speeds. The ridge is not as pronounces as it is in eagles or hawks.

The bills of falcons are unique. The upper mandibles or maxillas have a tomial tooth which corresponds with a notch in the lower mandibles. When the birds are biting prey, these two surfaces quickly and efficiently sever the spinal cords of their prey.

Male American Kestrel

Female American Kestrel

Orbital Ring

Tomial Tooth

Like pygmy-owls, Kestrels have false eye spots, or ocelli, on the backs of their heads. These false eyes may act as a deterrent from potential attackers that may strike the birds from behind; as the would-be assailant may think twice before attacking a Kestrel that may be actually watching the intruder. Predators are most successful when they make an attack on unsuspecting prey. If a predator makes an attack on prey that sees them coming, the prey will take evasive maneuvers to thwart the attack. If these attacks are impeded too often, the predators will starve.

American Kestrels false eye spots

Falcons have long toes with sharp claws, called talons. The undersides of their toes have rounded knobs called digital pads. These pads along with the bird's sharp talons enable falcons to maintain a firm grasp on their prey while both carrying it and feeding upon it.

American Kestrel's feet and talons

The eyesight of falcons, including American Kestrels is extraordinary. It is thought that they may be able to see six times more detail than humans. Their eyes also focus much faster than ours, as they must be able to discern detail while flying at high speeds. If you compare the size of a falcon's eyes, to the size of the bird itself, and do the same with us, you would see that a falcon's eyes are fifteen times larger than ours.

Falcon's eyes are spherical, and fixed in their skulls. Their eyes are so large that there is no room in their skulls for muscles to move their eyes. Furthermore, falcons have fifteen vertebras in their necks which enable them to look so far to the right that they can see over their backs.

Birds of prey, fish and amphibians have a third eyelid that covers each eye. This lid is called a nictitating membrane. It helps lubricate their eyes and protect them when attacking prey. When these creatures blink, you can see the membrane close over the eye a second or two before the upper and lower eyelids close. The nictitating membrane in birds closes from the upper inside corner of each eye to the outer lower corner.

Unlike us, American Kestrels, along with a few other bird species are thought to be able to see ultraviolet light. This aids Kestrels in detecting the urine trails left by small rodents. Mice and voles mark their territories with urine. The urine absorbs ultraviolet light. The Kestrels can see the urine streams and know these small mammals have been there. Thus, Kestrels simply perch in areas where they see these urine stains and wait for their prey to appear. Once their prey appears, the Kestrels make their attack and quickly dispatching the prey.

Male American Kestrel with a vole

Chapter Three

Habitat, Courtship and Nesting

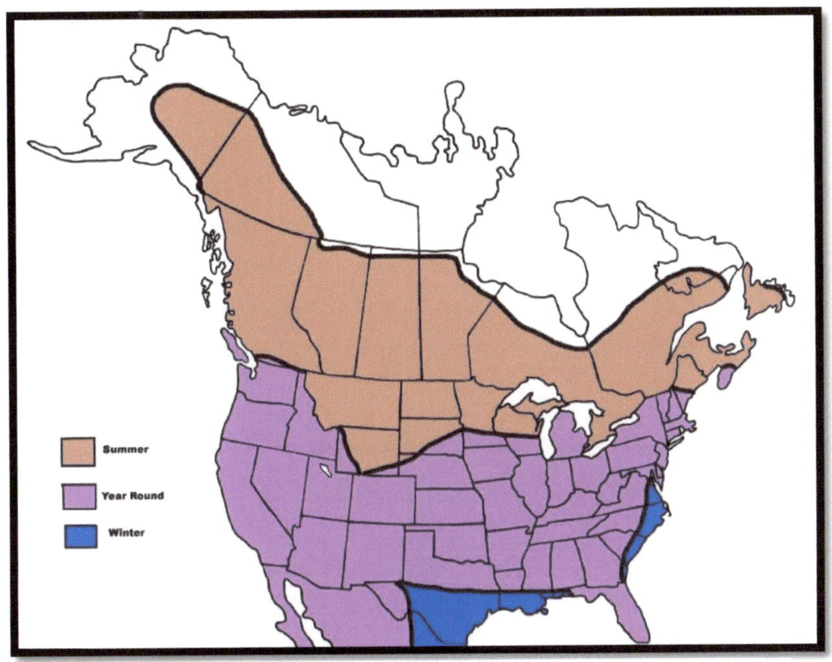

The range map of American Kestrels in North America

Habitat

American Kestrels can be found in open country including farmlands, urban yards, city parks and cemeteries. Their preferred habitat always has a nesting site, adequate prey, and several areas where the birds can perch while surveying for food.

Many Kestrel territories have powerlines within them that Kestrels perch on while surveying their territories. Powerlines make perfect perches for Kestrels because Kestrel's feet and talons fit perfectly around the wires.

When looking for American Kestrels, you may see Merlins, the Kestrel's larger cousins. Both species can be found in similar habitats, especially in the winter.

American Kestrels are easily discerned from Merlins, because Merlins frequently perch on telephone poles (below) rather than telephone wires. Merlins are stouter than Kestrels and subsequently cannot balance on wires as well. If a Merlin is perched on a wire, it is often sitting close to the pole where the wire is more taught. American Kestrels can balance easily on the thin wire.

A Merlin on a telephone pole

American Kestrels on wires (above and below)

**American Kestrel habitat; a large tree to perch on
and open country for hunting**

Rural American Kestrel habitat. Note the box on the pole (left)

Courtship

William Brewster in 1881 described the courtship of a pair of American Kestrels (Bent 1938) as follows…"To-day (sic) I saw them sitting not far apart on the tops of the neighboring dead balsams. Every now and then one, always the male, I thought, would mount high in the air to fly very rapidly, in a wide circle over and around where the other was perched, bending the tips of his wings downward and quivering them incessantly, at the same time uttering a shrill, clamorous *kee-kee cry*, oft (sic) repeated. Sometimes both would start off together, to chase another far and near, describing all manner of beautiful curves and occasionally sweeping down almost to the surface of the water. On realighting (sic) they invariably chose the very topmost twigs, often very slender ones, and settled on these with no less abruptness than precision, yet with admirable grace, scarce checking their speed until the perch was well-nigh (sic) reached and just then deftly folding their shapely wings."

Sherman C. Bishop (Bent 1938) watched a pair of American Kestrels for two weeks and described their courtship as follows: "Primarily to mating, the birds faced one another and slowly bobbed their heads and tails, the female keeping up a continuous low call." A few days later he watched them again and wrote; "Female called most of the afternoon. After mating, the male sometimes mount high in the air and preforms some remarkable evolutions-spirals, short dashes and a rapid drop ending on the back of the female."

Having cameras in our nest boxes enables us to watch additional portions of the American Kestrel's courtship activities.

Once the pair has accepted each other, the male will give his repetitive *klee, klee, klee* call, as he is flying to the nest that he wants the female to accept. He will fly into the cavity, or nest box, frequently calling as he enters. Once inside, he continues calling in hopes that she will follow him inside, which she frequently does. Both male and female will enter the nest one multiple occasions calling to each other. This tells other Kestrels that nest is taken.

If the male believes that its time for the female to begin laying eggs, he will enter the cavity with a vole, bird, or other morsel while vocalizing. He often leaves the morsel in the nest and exits. If she is not ready to nest she will take her food out of the nest and eat it elsewhere.

All of our nest boxes have a thin layer of wood shavings on the floor, which insures the eggs won't roll around in the box when the adults enter or leave rapidly. With wood shavings in our boxes, pairs take turns "making a scrape" on the floor of the box. Once adult birds enter a box, they lie on the floor and kick their feet backwards until they reach the bottom of the box. If the box was not cleaned from the previously year, the adults will still make a scrape, but it will be more shallow, as the packed nesting material is too solid for the birds to move.

After a nest site has been chosen, one and sometimes both adult Kestrels will sleep in the box at night. Other times the female will sleep in the box alone and the male will sleep in another location.

American Kestrels are a secondary cavity nesting species, which means that they need to nest in a cavity but are unable to construct one. They readily accept nest boxes that are placed in the proper habitat. If there are no nest boxes in the area, American Kestrels can be found nesting in abandoned Northern Flicker cavities, broken off branches in trees, holes in cliffs and on rare occasions, in abandoned Black-billed Magpie nests. We have learned that there is no need to place nest boxes any closer than three-quarters-of-a-mile apart, as Kestrels will frequently defend a territory that large.

Kestrel nest box in Eastern Colorado

Typical American Kestrel nest box on a pole

In 2017, after several days of rain, a friend told me that she had a pair of Kestrels nesting on a nest box in her front yard. We went to the property to see if eggs had been laid, and found five eggs inside the box on soaking wet bedding. The eggs were warm, as if the female had been incubating them.

Because the bedding was so wet, I decided to take out the eggs and the soggy bedding, and replaced the bedding with clean dry wood shavings. I then placed the eggs back in the box in the hopes that the female would feel better in a dry nest, and continue incubating her eggs; as I presumed that she was uncomfortable in a wet nest box.

I returned a week later to replace the old box with a new waterproofed one. However, when I looked inside the old box, I found that the female had abandoned her eggs. Two weeks later, the female was found in the back of the property incubating eggs under the eve of a loafing shed behind some pigeon spikes.

The loafing shed where a pair of American Kestrels nested

American Kestrel nestlings in the loafing shed behind pigeon spikes

American Kestrels have been known to raise their families in much larger nest boxes that were made for Wood Ducks, Rock Pigeons and Barn Owls. In both 2018 and 2020, American Kestrels nested in our Barn Owl boxes. Our Barn Owl nest boxes are much larger than the average Kestrel nest box, but the Kestrels seemed to enjoy themselves in these oversized structures.

D. Burkett (Cartron 2010) found a pair of Kestrels nesting in an unusual location in 2003. They had decided to nest in a yucca in a treeless area of New Mexico.

Kestrels occasionally nest in cavities created by Northern Flickers

Female American Kestrel nesting in a Barn Owl box

Chapter Four

Eggs

After the male and female American Kestrels have paired, determined their territory, and decided upon a nest site, the female begins laying eggs. American Kestrel eggs are oval-shaped and measure roughly 35 mm x 28 mm. They vary in color from light brown with dark brown spots; to almost white with light rusty spots.

The female American Kestrel lays an average of five eggs. However, we have seen as few as two and as many as ten eggs in a single nest.

At times, other birds including Northern Flickers and European Starlings will nest in American Kestrel boxes (page 35).

Average clutch size of American Kestrels

Unusual clutches sizes of American Kestrel eggs (above and below)

Color variations of American Kestrel eggs (above and below)

Some females will remain within their nest boxes appearing lethargic a day to a few days prior to laying their first egg.

European Starling eggs (left) and Northern Flicker eggs (right) can occasionally be found in Kestrel boxes

Incubation

The female lays one egg every two days or so. Some females will begin incubating when the first or second egg is laid, yet others will not being incubating until they have finished laying all of their eggs. Some females Kestrels will guard their nests during the day and sleep in them at night. When sleeping in their nests, they sleep next to the eggs, so not to start incubating them. Other females will leave their eggs completely unprotected, even sleeping away from the nest at night, and returning to begin incubating once all of their eggs are laid.

Kestrel eggs, a nestling and an individual that has just finished exiting its egg

Still other females will partially incubate their eggs as they lay them. They spend a portion of the day sitting on their eggs, and another portion of the day hunting and preening.

After all the eggs are laid and incubation begins, the male and female take turns incubating. The male will frequently incubate for a couple of hours each day, while the female hunts for herself. Incubation lasts between 29 and 32 days. In some cases, all the eggs will hatch on the same day and in other cases the eggs will hatch over a two or three day period.

Female Kestrel incubating her eggs

Growth of nestling American Kestrels

It takes young American Kestrels about six hours to exit their eggs. When hatched, nestlings are wet and covered with white down. Their eyes are closed and their eye lids are pink as is their beak, legs and feet (page 36). Once out of the shell, they can open their eyes for a few seconds at a time. After the third day, they are capable of keeping their eyes open.

Female Kestrels will offer their chicks small pieces of meat as soon as they are completely out of their shells. When the females place food near her chicks' faces, they readily eat.

Female feeds her nestlings before they can open their eyes

When the nestlings are four days old and older, they can see their parents enter their nests and instantly begin food begging.

The chicks grow rapidly, and when they are nine days old, you can discern males from females by looking at their wing feathers. Male Kestrels have slate blue-gray upper wing coverts, and females have rust-colored upper wing coverts. Ideally, we band our nestlings after they are nine days old or older, because at that age, we can discern the sexes.

The wing of a nestling American Kestrel. The dark lines point to the brown wing feathers that denotes a female

Male American Kestrel nestling above. Both male and female American Kestrel below; male left, female right

American Kestrels remain within their nests for about a month before fledging. During this time, both parents will deliver food to the nestlings.

Adult female feeding week-old nestlings (above). Three week old nestlings (below)

Male and female American Kestrels a few days before fledging.
The male is on the left

Nestling American Kestrel about to fledge

Fledgling female American Kestrel

Chapter Five

Prey and Hunting

American Kestrels prey upon insects, reptiles, amphibians, small mammals and small birds. Their diet varies upon time of year, and nesting location. In the northern portions of their range, I have witnessed wintering American Kestrels prey upon small mammals such as mice and voles, and occasionally larger prey including gophers. Some of the birds which they commonly take are House Sparrows, House Finches and Horned Larks.

I have witnessed Kestrels with prey several times during the winter. At that time of year, American Kestrels routinely prey upon voles and mice, European Starlings, Horned Larks, Lapland Longspurs, House Finches, Snow Buntings, American Goldfinches and House Sparrows.

Kestrels that nest on grasslands of Northern Colorado feed heavily upon grasshoppers, beetles, horned lizards, voles and mice, and Horned Larks, Vesper's Sparrows, Savannah Sparrows, Brewer's Sparrows, McCowen's and Chestnut-sided Longspurs.

Kestrels that nest in the mountains of Northern Colorado feed upon voles and mice and birds including Audubon's Warblers, Vesper's Sparrows, House Sparrows, Pine Siskins and House Finches.

Nesting birds in the foothills of Northern Colorado fed upon dragon flies and other flying insects, grasshoppers, beetles, small snakes, lizards, mice, voles, Tree Swallows, House Sparrows, House Finches, Vesper's Sparrows and European Starlings.

In 1918, Dr. Bryant in Bent (1938) found American Kestrels in California fed upon black crickets, white-footed mice, Jerusalem crickets, and grasshoppers.

Kestrels feed upon deer mice (above) and voles (below)

E.A. Smyth (1912) in Bent (1938) found American Kestrels in Virginia fed upon House Sparrows, crickets and one that killed and fed upon a fledgling American Robin.

Female American Kestrel about to eat a vole that it just captured

Female American Kestrel with a half-eaten vole

F H. Allen (Bent 1938) found a Kestrel feeding upon a small snake. P. Bonnet (Bent 1938) tells of a Sparrow Hawk (American Kestrel) which "sailed gently to one of the [cliff] swallow's nests, passing over a group of about fifteen people, supported himself with one foot, hanging nearly upside-down in the meantime, inserted the other foot into the nest, and extracted the owner. The captured bird was an adult Cliff Swallow. The nest was not very deep, and the opening was large."

Floyd Bralliar (Bent 1938) described the scene of an American Kestrel making a kill. "The hawk (sic) watches until he feels sure of his prey, then swoops downward straight as an arrow, strikes the bird in the back with its talons, and with his powerful beak tears the top of the head off. The point of the beak is sunk into the base of the skull, and the skull is torn off with a swift forward motion."

George M. Wright (Bent 1938) witnessed an America Kestrel make an unusual kill. "The hawk (sic) flew low over the edge of the plateau, and while under observation it was seen to be pursuing a small fluttering object which I instantly took to be a bird. My immediate thought was to make sure that it was a sparrow hawk (sic) thus engaging in so unorthodox a pursuit. My field glasses were trained on the hawk and followed it while it dived at its prey, which proved to be a small bat. It dived repeatedly, not following the bat about, but striking at it and then gaining a little height before bearing down again. Once, however, it followed the bat into the overhanging recess toward which it was retreating and chased it out again. At about the seventh attempt, the little bat was caught in its talons and carried to the top of the ledge over the recess. The bird remained there for about two minutes, picked at its prize a couple of times and then flew to a rock on the plateau above."

I have witnessed American Kestrels hunting several times during the nesting season. When hunting ground dwelling prey such as grasshoppers and voles, Kestrels frequently do so from an exposed perch such as a powerline, bare limb or roof of a structure. They perch for extended periods of time scanning the ground until a prey shows itself.

Another technique American Kestrels use when searching for prey is hovering. Hovering allows Kestrels to remain in the air, essentially motionless, while search the ground for prey. The act of hovering occurs as the bird glides into the wind and flaps at the same speed that the wind is blowing. The bird's long tail is opened somewhat and tilted slightly downward. All of this together stops the bird from any forward movement.

Once prey is spotted, either from a perch or while hovering, the Kestrel dives head-first at its prey. Just before impact, its feet come forward and grasp the unsuspecting prey. The Kestrel then bites the creature in the back of its head, killing it instantly. It frequently flies to a perch to consume its meal. If the bird is nesting, it will take the prey to the nestlings.

Food Caching

Falcons and owls, along with a few other groups of birds, frequently capture more prey than they can consume. When this occurs, they often hoard or cache the excess. Caching frequently occurs prior to inclement weather. I believe that birds can feel the barometric pressure change before a storm moves in.

Years ago, a friend of mine operated a bird rehabilitation center in Broomfield. Each morning, a male American Kestrel would routinely arrive at her facility. When she saw the bird, she would toss a dead mouse on the roof of one of the buildings and the Kestrel would come in, take the mouse and fly off.

One morning, just before a snowstorm was to arrive, she threw a mouse on the roof for the Kestrel. The Kestrel came in, took the mouse, and flew off. This particular morning, the bird returned for seconds. She threw a second mouse on the roof. The kestrel took that mouse and flew off, as it has done previously. It came back a third time, and she threw a third mouse to it. When the Kestrel came back the fourth time, she told it to hunt for itself.

The interesting part was that while it was snowing, the bird was absent. However, after the storm had passed and the weather warmed up, the Kestrel returned. It was presumed that the bird was staying out of site during the storm and eating what it had cached.

Pellets

As mentioned earlier, American Kestrels are meat eaters. When eating, they hold their prey with their feet and talons, tearing off pieces with their sharp beaks and swallowing.

The food goes down the esophagus and enters the crop. It is held there prior to entering the stomach. Once in the stomach, digestion occurs. The indigestible portions of the prey, including scales, feather, fur and wings (of insects) is formed in a pellet and regurgitated roughly six hours after being swallowed.

Kestrel pellets are quite small, about the size of a penny, or smaller. By dissecting a Kestrel pellet, one learns exactly what the bird has consumed.

Kestrel pellets with a penny for size (above)
Dissected pellet with a penny for size (below)

Chapter Six

Mortality

American Kestrels, along with all other birds of prey are protected by state and federal law. However, this was not always the case. There was a time when all predatory birds were considered vermin and collected (shot) for private collections as well as collected in the name of research.

American Kestrels have met their demise in a variety of circumstances. Some crash into windows, while hunting near homes, because birds have no concept of windows. When they see the reflection in the window, they believe they can fly in that direction and subsequently crash into it and crack or crush their skulls. Occasionally Kestrels get hit by cars while hunting near roads and highways. They get so focused on their prey that they don't see or hear the automobiles approaching. Wind turbines have caused the death of many birds including American Kestrels. When the birds are in flight searching for prey, they simply looking down and fly into the moving blades.

Habitat loss such as converting agricultural fields to housing developments can contribute to fewer nesting sites. This often brings a greater use of pesticides that can cause a reduction in reproduction of adult Kestrels and mortality of both adult and nestling Kestrels. Predation by larger raptors including Cooper's Hawks, Great Horned Owls and Red-tailed Hawks, along with house cats is another cause of mortality in American Kestrels. American Kestrels are also susceptible to diseases including West Nile Virus and Trichomoniasis.

The Fish and Wildlife Service found that several species of birds including American Kestrels met their demise while falling down uncapped vertical pipes that are spread across the landscape for the release of household gases. American Kestrels have starved and died after entering a structure and being unable to find their way out.

By far the most unusual reason for American Kestrel mortality was documented in North-central Saskatchewan. Researchers found cannibalism by both the nesting bird's parents and their siblings.

Unexplained Deaths

In 2019, we found dead Kestrels in three of our nest boxes near Longmont. We presumed the birds consumed small mammals that had previously consumed poison. In the nests we found all of the nestlings dead.

In Fort Collins, we found a single dead nestling in a nest box after its four siblings had fledged. Unfortunately, we were unable to have it tested because it was too decomposed when we found it.

We have three Kestrel nest boxes near the Wyoming border along a dirt road. One box fledged six Kestrels, another fledged three Kestrels and the third had five dead Kestrels inside. As the previous birds, these were also too decomposed to have a necropsy preformed. Therefore their cause of death was undetermined.

Longevity

According to the Bird banding Laboratory, the oldest wild American Kestrel lived to be 13 years, 7 months old.

Rehabilitation of Kestrels

In many places in North America, the American Kestrels are one of the most frequently injured birds of prey. There are many reasons why Kestrels end up at rehabilitation centers. Examples are attacks by dogs and house cat attacks, crashing into windows, getting stuck in barbed wire fences, or being poisoned. Some get attacked by larger birds, including American Crows, Black-billed Magpies, Steller's Jays and Blue Jays.

In 1994, a male and a female American Kestrel were brought to me to be rehabilitated. The female fledged her nest and flew directly into a car. It was very fortunate that someone was there to both watch her fledge, and pick her up before she was run over by a passing automobile. After I examined her, I found that she had a broken humorous and was blind*. The humorous is one of the two bones that stretch from the elbow to the wrist. Because there are two bones that are petty-much side-by-side, when one bone is broken, and the other is not; the unbroken bone acts as a splint to immobilize the broken bone long enough for it to heal. This works well as long as the bird can keep the injured wing immobile.

It took about a week and a half for the broken wing to heal, but the blindness was a different story. The Kestrel's eyesight returned in her left eye, but she remained blind in her right.

Before her eyesight returned, I hand fed her small pieces of cut up mouse, twice a day, until she could feed herself. I named her Katie. *I knew that Katie was blind because when I tried to feed her she made no attempt to take the food that was placed in front of her. I would have to open her mouth and place the food behind her tongue. After a short while, she would start biting the air trying to figure out where the food was.

A few weeks after Katie's arrival, I received a male Kestrel that had a wing so badly broken that is could not heal properly. I named him Spike. I eventually, placed the pair in my flight cage where they spent 16 months together. Katie could fly and would eat two mice per day and the Spike could not fly would eat a single mouse each day. Because I have only a single flight cage, I needed to take the pair to the Birds of Prey Foundation, in Broomfield where they lived together for several years before succumbing to West Nile virus.

Male American Kestrel

American Kestrel Nest Box Design

American Kestrel Nest Box

Front: 11 x 16 inches (27.94 cm x 40.64 cm)

Back: 11 x 22 inches (27.94 x 55.88 cm)

Side: 11 x 16 inches (27.94 cm x 40.64 cm)

Side: 7 x 9 inches (Door on side) (17.78 cm x 22.86 cm)

Side Bottom: 7 x 7 inches (17.78 cm x 17.78 cm)

Top: 11 x 13 inches (27.94 x 33.02 cm)

Bottom: 11 x 9.5 inches (27.94 cm x 24.13 cm)

Entrance Hole: 3 inches (7.62 cm)

Bibliography:

Bent A.C. 1938 Life Histories of North American Birds of Prey. Part Two.99-127.

Berg. C. 2004. From hunter to hunted* Decline of American Kestrels linked to predation by Cooper's Hawks. Morning Call newspaper.

Bortolotti. G. R.,et al. 1991. Cannibalism of nestling American Kestrels by their parents and siblings. Canadian Journal of Zoology.69(6): 1447-1453.

Cartron. J-L.E. Raptors of New Mexico. pp. 393-413.

Davis. K. 2008. Falcons of North America.

Patla, S.M. et.al. Wyoming Species Account. American Kestrel *Falco sparverious* . pp. 1-7.

Smallwood, K.S. and The Lander, C.G. Bird Mortality at the Altamont Pass Wind Resource Area March 1998-September 2001. National Renewable Energy Laboratory. pp. 288.

U.S. Fish and Wildlife Service. 2018. Death by Pipe.

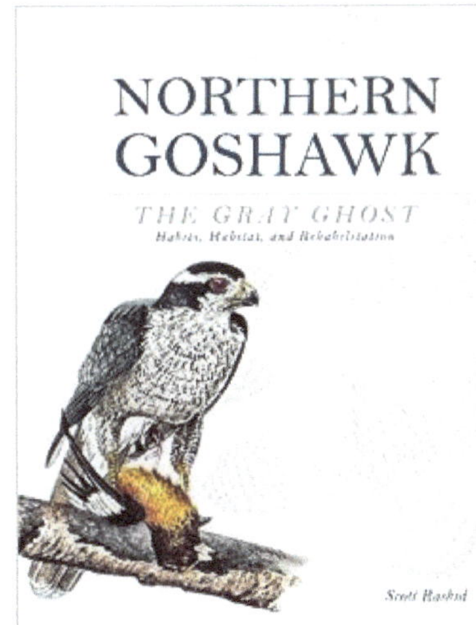

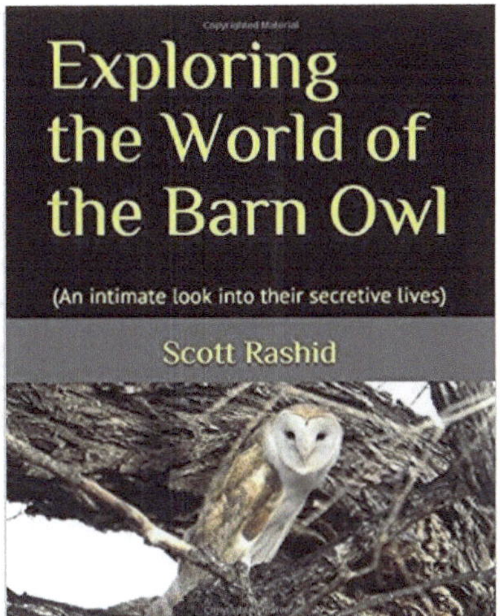